Purposefully Unintentional

Poems by Jas Abramowitz

Kansas City   Spartan Press   Missouri

Spartan Press
Kansas City, Missouri
spartanpresskc.com

Copyright (c) Jason Abramowitz, 2018
First Edition 1 3 5 7 9 10 8 6 4 2
ISBN: 978-1-946642-77-6
LCCN: 2018960655

Design, edits and layout: Jason Ryberg
Cover image: Elizabeth Hershey
Author photos: Andrew B. Carroll, Leni Manaa-Hopenworth
All rights reserved. No part of this publication may be
reproduced or transmitted in any form or by any means,
electronic or mechanical, including photocopying,
recording or by info retrieval system, without prior
written permission from the author.

Spartan Press would like to thank Prospero's Books, The Fellowship of N-finite Jest, The Prospero Institute of Disquieted P/o/e/t/i/c/s, Will Leathem, Tom Wayne, Jeanette Powers, j. d. tulloch, Jon Bidwell, Jason Preu, Mark McClane, Tony Hayden and the whole Osage Arts Community.

Author acknowledgements:

I would like to extend very special thanks to the following amazing people: Storm Johnson, Tyler Rowe, Sherry Abramowitz, Beth O'bryan, Robin Abramowitz- You all are my rocks- Thanks for all the shoes.

To Spartan Press and Duke Walter- this book exists and is better because of you- Thanks!

To Elizabeth, Damon, Mark, Freedom, Doug, Blick- FUYB.

To Dolly Johnson- my love, my life, my entirety- you make everything possible.

CONTENTS

Blah Blah Blah / 1

Face Value / 4

3000 Years / 5

Cheffing / 6

Taste / 8

Food Addict / 10

Salmonella / 11

'Tis the Season / 12

Summer Poem / 15

Sports Alliterated / 17

Boxing Is / 20

Barstool Contemplation / 21

Buzzard Beach / 22

Flirty Girls / 25

Getting Fucked Up / 26

Rise / 27

Crank / 28

Zebra Mind / 29

What Doesn't Kill You / 30

Aversion / 32

In Howling Season / 34

Hunter / 35

This Skin / 38

Dan Suelo / 42

Release / 43

Idiot Wind / 44

Sharing Air / 45

Master Plan / 48

Dead End / 50

Thirst / 52

Love Poem #69 / 54

April Fool #3 / 55

Maria / 56

April Fool #1 / 57

Not Zombie Love / 58

Time Study / 59

Olfactory Musings / 61

Color by Numbers / 64

What Have I Done / 66

April Fool #5 / 67

April Fool #4 / 69

April Fool #6 / 70

Deadbeat / 71

A Poem for My Mother / 72

Deadbeat #2 / 75

Our Story / 76

This book is dedicated to my family, both of blood and choice, without whom, this book would not have been possible.

Blah Blah Blah

The words,
I regurgitate
like some sort of poetic bulimia,
spilling out of me,
deposited
on great, tanned, parchment gods.

The words,
discolored with simile,
half-digested chunks of metaphor,
and last nights juxtaposition
mingle and dance in the
less than sterile
canine drinking bowl.
Because there are some things
which need not be said,
and those are summarily ejected
from my body, from my mind.

For those words,
strung together
like beads,
or panels of a quilt,
which do see the light of day,
which are not
flushed or
burned—

I eat them.
I eat them and shit them out,
here in this public forum
for everyone to inspect and critique.

Yes, you'll say,
that poem had corn in it,
and it smells foul,
but there's something to it.

Later that night,
you'll find yourself
submersed in the stink of my words.
If only I could get those words out of my nose,
you'll think to yourself,
but the stink will remain.

There is only one way
to properly digest poetry
and that is to chew.
Thirty-six times you have to take the words in your mouth.
Thirty-six times you have to feel them squish between your teeth.
Thirty-six times you have to feel them slide down your throat.

And then once you have properly digested the poem
you can look anyone in the face
and say:
Eat me.
Eat my poem.
Eat my words.
Chew on this!

Face Value

These words pass by you
and your eyes eat them ravenously
insatiable, systemic, grotesque.
You search for deeper meaning in these words
or you simply feign aptitude (that's what I do),
but my words are face-value.

I am not advanced. I am status quo.
Fuck off, eat shit, drop dead.
See if I give a shit.

3000 years

Sun down
desert scape
across the borders
they drop bombs.

Wrapped in a veil
personal hell
Children of Israel
they drop bombs.

Planes scream overhead
people on both sides
they drop dead.
Same fight
Same fears
Same tears
Three Thousand years.

Cheffing

When I was a chef,
I always looked at my food like poetry.

Pouring my heart into something
so beautiful.
Tenderly, I would arrange it on the plate.
Just a pinch of parsley for decoration,
a splash of olive oil,
a ladle of bechamel,
a pinch of salt and pepper.

I wasn't just manufacturing food.
I was creating art,
and there was no greater honor
than seeing an empty plate.
No greater honor
than knowing
something I so lovingly created,
inspired someone
to destroy it completely.

It is like
seeing the Mona Lisa
and being so overtaken by its beauty
you had no choice but to
rip it to shreds.

When I was a chef,
I always looked at my food like poetry.

The pizza
with its grease running from head to foot,
like rivers running through channels,
or
roasted chicken
with the perfect jus,
shining on a plate
like a jewel.

Anybody can make a meal,
but it takes a Chef
to cook poetry.

Taste

I peel the covering, slowly.
Piece by piece,
layer by layer,
revealing the fruit
which lies underneath.
Sweet and juicy
my tongue relishes
the sweet nectar.
The juices running down my face
so that I must wipe my chin,
smear the liquid into my beard,
before I go back for seconds
and I always go back for seconds.
Because something that sweet
must be enjoyed and savored,
drop by succulent drop,
again and again.
For when the fruit is ripe
it is a visceral example of
lust and sensuality.
Still, it's a matter of timing,
isn't it?
Like relationships,
unripened fruit
too often
turns sour,

leaving faces to cringe,
and nectar wasted,
my beard dry,
the plate
empty and cold.

Should I simply say
I would trade all of the unripened fruit
I may one day taste
for one single night
of the sweetest juice
running down my chin
relishing the ripeness
again and again.

Food Addict

I'm addicted to food.
I can't live without it.
It's like my body goes
through withdrawal if I don't have it.
I went to a psychotherapist.
I said, *Doctor, I'm addicted to food
isn't there a 12 step program for this?*
The therapist said,
You know you have to eat to survive, don't you?
WELL, FUCK.
What am I going to do now?
I went to a dietician.
I said, *Dietician... I'm addicted to food.*
She said, *You know, you have to eat to survive.*
WELL, FUCK.
I said,
What the hell?
America is the fattest nation in the world
and you're telling me, I HAVE to eat?
There's no twelve step program?

Salmonella

Eggs
Baby Chickens, I say.
I've said it before.
Chickens giving birth.
Having their children
torn away from them.

Baby Chickens
never allowed
to breathe,
to eat,
to shit,
to think,
to die?

Like ripping a two month old fetus out of the womb.
Fried, scrambled or over-easy?
Whoa,
Salmonella.

'Tis the Season

'Tis the season.
When the weather first
Shoves the fat, moist cock of summer
right in our faces.

Everyone in the Midwest knows
'round these parts, 't'aint the heat.

It's as if
Father Time
with his wrinkly skin and old balls,
bored with the rhythmic nothingness of forever,
chooses to waste his days romancing
Mother Nature.

With every passing hour his temperature rises,
flustered by the chase,
until finally she submits.
A sticky wet eon passes,
the staccato slap of their meat smacking flesh
beholds the unholy offspring of humidity.
He should have taken her ass.

Round these parts
people describe the air as thick,
people describe the heat as wet.

'Tain't summer 'less'n y'break out in sweat walkin to th'car.
'T'ain't summer 'less'n when ya breathe feels like ya got a brick on yer face.
Just 't'aint summer 'less steppin outside to smoke leaves you feelin' sticky as a two dollar whore on half-price night hosting a bachelor party gang bang.

The unholy child wreaks havoc on the world. Mother Nature, sensing the discontent of her flock,
understanding she has become Grendel's mother, knows she must give it a spin.
Use it to her advantage.
In an act of biological warfare
she uses her monster to
force everyone inside,
protected by Holy Air Conditioning,
transfixed by blue lights and backlights and bright screens,
as if we were all on heroin.
Empty-eyed zombies
stuck inside, wasting our destiny.

Father Time,
always distracted with the business of eternity,
never one to see his errors,
having lived long enough to
watch consequences pass into nothing,
finally understands, his whorish ways, fueled by boredom,
undid him in the end.

His bane, an accepted piece of the midwestern fabric,
weaved into midwestern culture.

Round these parts
just 't'aint summer without humidity.

Mother Nature, understanding the nature of all things,
including mankind,
smiles,
wipes the sweat from her brow,
and waits for fall.

Summer Poem

Summer sweat drips from forehead to feet.
Oppressive fumes rise from concrete like steam
from a tea kettle.
It's so fucking hot out,
it makes me want to shove a screwdriver in my eyeball
and scream
You don't EVER tell me what to do!
Which may not seem that unusual until I realize
I'm screaming at the fire hydrant.
Staring at me with its judging eyes.
All painted and full of water.
Stupid fire hydrant.
I'd much rather be cold.
Strap on an extra coat, build a bigger fire.
When it's this hot out,
you can only go so long
before you're naked
in a tub of ice water
and still sweating
like your sitting at the dinner table
on the fourth level of hell
with nothing to eat but fried okra
and nothing to do
but answer the same question
over and over again

from your dead grandma up in heaven
who insists on repeatedly asking,
how's the weather, it must be warm down there?
You don't EVER tell me it's warm down here!
Stupid Grandma.
The main thing I hate about the stewing, sweat
inducing, salacious summer is it makes me irritable.
But fuck, I don't want to move.
I just want to exist in my pool of palpable perspiration
and bitch about the heat.
Stupid heat,
always judging me with its judging eyes.
Where the hell's my tub of ice water?

Sports Alliterated

Steven pondered the pennant.
Seven seasons he sat on the sawed seat
and surprised when suddenly selected to start.

Steven Shaw- starting shortstop.
(he read it in the paper, it had to be true)

His numbered jersey he thought nifty,
tucked neatly into his knickers,
his knee-high socks nearly nestled into his
nether regions.

Reasons rarely reversed his reverence -
undrafted and dealt two times.
Determined not to be indifferent,
daily he worked diligently to develop.

Genetics jeopardized
and giant obstacles,
and jeering crowds,
and jittery nerves,
his job was in jeopardy,
so he jammed his veins with juice.

Steroids made him stronger.
Steroids surged the speed of his swing.

He bashed baseballs over far fences.
The finicky fans of the nation noticed,
and Steven Shaw seemed a star.

He hit homers at a horrifying rate.
Soon he blasted Babe,
murdered Maris,
moved Mcgwire's mark,
and buried Bonds
standing solitary to the sports most sacred standard.

But the brighter his buzz burned,
the better it packed a pulverizing pressure.
He pined for the past,
playing in the park,
kicking up dust.
Back when he was a skinny shaver.
Before treatments turned task into talent.

Perception was perfection,
but within he was withered,
a marginal man,
meager and insecure,
his single selection to shoot up.

His body, busted and bested
he succumbed
and could not recover.

His star shone bright—
but burned out,
became a supernova,
disappeared.

Steven never knew
with each bang,
be it a homer or vein,
his soul suffocated,
until he was withered.

Steven was never selected
or came close to Cooperstown
He perished as an asterisk.

Boxing Is

Boxing
        is
moving,
it's punching,
it's footwork,
it's dodging, it's shaking,
it's 6AM at the park on Saturday
   practicing moves.
It's trying to move faster
   than your shadow.
It's the slap and dust of a lonesome punching bag.
The early morn chill
       does not discourage.
   6AM Saturday practicing moves,
practicing movement,
      ballet,
         poetry.
Boxing is movement, it's ballet,
   it's poetry,
      it's 6 AM Saturday commitment,
it's moving quicker than your shadow,
      and hoping your shadow is quicker than your opponents.
Boxing is
   the poetry
      of movement.

Barstool Contemplation

At the bar,
time for lonely contemplation.
What in life, what is life?
Anything can be figured out with enough cold beers
and warm cigarettes.
At the bar,
the clearness of day, the serenity of peaceful night
and the mellow of booze
are juxtaposed.
Here sport and weather are king!
A hot meal is just a smile away.
At the bar,
you can find beer, booze, food and love,
drink until you have problems,
or drink until your problems disappear,
but at the bar,
problems don't exist.
Nothing exists, except you, your drink, and the cool
of the bar underneath your elbows.

Buzzard Beach

Buzzard Beach
things are quiet now.
I'm here every Tuesday and Thursday
because I'm dating the bartender.
Cool, sexy, can do math
and crazy.

Dating this bartender is dangerous,
She is locally infamous.
Sure, there are perks.
Alcohol, well known for its stupid-inducing effects,
can cause wild, emerald behaviors.
A pinch of jealousy and youth,
The danger becomes palpable.

9PM
the game starts curiously early.
Pheromones ride the air particles.
Predator women,
drunk and stumbley,
meander upon my table.
Unnaturally blond hair
compliments her pomegranate red eyes
Slurring her intent
Do I want to party later?
I am resolute.

11PM
Location change
downstairs
through the gauntlet
of drunken rage and tobacco
two doe types
flutter and wink
tongues wetting lips.
I coax stability
from the wooden shaft of the pool cue,
every ounce of it.
I am resolute.

1AM
One and one quarter gallons
Inhibitions destroying limbo.
Everyone is beautiful,
I want to know them.
Some want to know me.
Contemplation interrupted,
evil glances from behind the bar
declination with a condition
number in my phone
under
party.
I am resolute.

2AM
Entire city arrives.
The pool, infinitely larger.
Mating rituals commence.
Orange moon hangs low in the sky,
aggression abounds,
resolution deteriorating,
shrill screams from behind the bar
eyes twinkling,
dark look about her.
Last call declared!
Sweet Victory!
Crisis averted.

9PM Future

Buzzard Beach
things are quiet.
I'm here every Tuesday,
because I used to date the bartender.
She's angry, hot, did the math,
logical.

Alcohol, well known for its stupid-inducing effects,
can cause wild, emerald behaviors.
A pinch of jealousy and youth,
The danger becomes unavoidable.

Flirty Girls

Goddamn,
pretty,
boyfriend-having,
flirty girls!
They drive me crazy as they coo at you in bar.
You knowing, they knowing they have another.
Yet, she stares in your eyes and smiles. Occasionally
makes a subtle comment or some light contact,
which is obvious enough to be smelled by the dog
across the street.
She even jokingly propositions you
and you know if you could beat up the boyfriend,
but you know you can't,
so you don't,
and it's over
and you go home
and think,
goddamn,
pretty,
boyfriend-having,
flirty girls!

Getting Fucked Up

Getting fucked up boy!
Scotch Whiskey and Green Bud.
Girl lay on the floor, she so fucked up.
I'm heading out the door, cause, man. I am fucked up!
I got an idea, let's go to the store… taking the car!
Another drink, another puff, another snort.
I got an idea let's take out the car!
Got to make it till the sun comes up.
Can I make it till the sun comes up?
I gotta make it till the sun comes up!

Rise

On the way up
manifest in my brain
warm the cheeks hot
sunshine cheeks
Smile creep across my face uncontrollably
permagrinned
feeling
remarkably in a neutral
kind of way
Show me light
to lead to the golden pathway
to eternal love
To ethereal orgy
To cumming clouds
on god's big face
and don't ask me anything
i can't answer directly
Yes, God has a lawyer
and his name
is Michael.

Crank

Sleep
If I don't sleep
I'm in a heap
and
trouble
'cause what that means is
I gots some white powder
in my jeans pocket
and that I ain't eating
And you know what that means
don't you?

Zebra Mind

Crystal Methane in the vein,
plunger stops the hunger.
Shot up again today.
Bruise on my arm; eyes glued open, thoughts glide by,
grazing the surface.
Sleep beckons only as a pattern.
Lay down, let darkness fall.
Consume me Night!
Take away the impurity of day!
I shall look no one in the face today,
for I cannot face the fact that today
I lied to myself,
and weakness prevailed like a sick zebra
escaping a pack of lions

What Doesn't Kill You

Every pack of smokes I buy,
I am reminded,
that this is bad, and it's going to kill me.

Every liquid libation containing caffeine and alcohol,
that touches my parted lips,
I am reminded,
that this is bad, and it's going to kill me.

Every time I use a chemical
for its sociologically unintended purpose,
and it makes me feel good,
I am reminded,
that this is bad, and it's going to kill me.

Every time I consume red meat
cooked to perfection in hot oil,
I am reminded,
no matter how good it tastes,
that this is bad, and it's going to kill me.

Every time I lay around,
get in a vehicle,
have unprotected sex,
walk to get to any location,
breathe air,

I am reminded
that this is bad, and it's going to kill me.

Well guess what?
I'm alive and this, my friends,
is what's going to kill me.

Aversion

It's not that I need the drugs
to make my heart flutter and spin my stomach in circles.

I don't, necessarily, need to smoke the weed
to make my head swell with intoxicating excitement.

It's not that I need the cigarettes
to feel that smoldering closeness.

It's waking up at 2am with her next to me,
warming the bed with the heat of naked flesh,
breathing heavy and heavier still the gravity with which
I am bound to her,

It's not that I need to get high
to feel elevated by the closeness of her.

I don't necessarily need to drink
to be slushy and satiated.

It's going to bed at 9pm with her next to me,
warming the bed with the heat of our naked flesh
that gets me loaded.

It's not that I need to get hammered.

When she is holding my hand and looking up at me,
I'm in as good of a place as I have ever been.

It's not that I have an aversion to intemperance,
because girl, when we get stoned and combine
our genitals,
I'm taken to a new universe, shifted consciousness
trans-dimensionally to a place where the entire reality
consists of her and I and the edacious way we ravage
each other with wolfish somber.
A universe where we are the drug and reality
doesn't require an escape.

It's not that I need the drugs
to get lit
Life's just more fun,
when they're in it.

In Howling Season

Coyote
searches for his mate
    with yelping whines
guided only by scent, moon's light,
the loch, the thicket, the foliage.

He calls out to her
  hoping she will respond to his desperate whines.

Coyote born into the world blind and helpless,
  a shadow,
      a whisper,
           a memory of days past,
he must depend on his pack to survive.

Coyote.
Fur, bones, blood and teeth
Moon, brush, lake and pack.

In howling season,
we yell to the moon.

Coyote!
We are not so different you and I.

Hunter

In the wild days of yonder
amongst the survivalist tribes
When man was still animal
We were hunters.
Other species, our mentors
Lions, Wolves, Vultures.

In the wild days of present
amongst the populus mass
where man is king,
what type of hunter am I?
Which is my mentor?
If I am authentic to present
Would I be an empathetic lion?

Apologies Zebra
You do not desire
to die by the cut of my teeth
gnawing at your flesh
until your life is released.
But among your herd,
you are the weak,
prone to disease.
My hunger designed
to save your species.

So I give you thanks.
Shrug my shoulders
and feast.

What lessons would a wolf teach?
The cave, the pack, to each
one beholden, to share the feast,
to howl in moonlight.

A vulture would show
how to live left over,
nothing to waste,
no ally of haste.
A life I could sow,
if not for the rotten distaste.

If the wild days of present
were truly kingdom,
if man were still animal,
would we still rule?
Still be the jewel
on the food chain crown?
Who would be your mentor?
The lion, the wolf, or the vulture?

There is only one mentor
with the ability to teach this fool
and that is the bull.

There is no violence
to graze on grass,
to find a lass, move across the sea
to India,
begin a family.

In the wild days of present,
our animal mentor obsolete.
Survival of the fittest?
The new arithmetic,
survival of the richest.

The cliches are true
on what money cannot buy
but it can purchase
a ton of guns.
Let's enjoy extinction.

This Skin

This skin,
which covers my bones and makes up my face, my flesh,
my physical carapace,
which keeps my energy bound to this earth,
so I may walk in the footsteps of my ancestors,
the monkeys.

This skin,
which used to be dark not light,
in a time when there was no meaning
for words like white or black,
one only had to worry about whether snakes would attack,
so we moved up to the trees, that's where we developed these opposable thumbs.
They say, are the catalyst for evolution,
caused us to lose our hair,
grow bigger brains,
that's how we began our ascent from that place until we moved beyond the food chain.
One race,
the human race,
was once unified as we strived to evolve.

What happened to us?
Why did we go from fight together to fight each other?
When did this skin change from dark to light?

It happened roughly thirty thousand years before
the birth of Christ,
when the first human beings began to mutate with
phenotypical traits,
including genetic recessive,
blonde hair,
blue eyes,
white skin,
which was a sin against the original man,
who we now call African.
Some of those mutants moved north of the equator,
we called them Europeans later,
they became the first race haters,
as the unified skin of the human being,
split and mutated
like the branches of the trees
where we developed these (opposable thumbs).

We used this skin to separate us from nature,
we called ourselves homo sapiens later.
Said we no longer had to live by that order,
and found ourselves killing each other,
like a bunch of goddamn fools, for what?
For race,
from hate,
no longer unified,
isn't it great?

This skin,
became
a source of pain,
a source of control,
a way to differentiate,
a broader defined role from which culture substantiates,
manifesting in rapes, in war, in deaths.

This skin,
which ties me to a culture of hate,
a culture of rape,
a culture of money hungry, power hungry,
megalomaniacal primates.

This skin,
which covers our bones and makes up our face,
our flesh,
our physical carapace,
which binds our energy to the earth,
which allow us woe and bliss,
which holds the chemical formula of emotion,
which houses such devotion for creationism versus
education, are we fucking joking?

This is what we lost our claws for?
This is why we came down from the trees?
This is what we abandoned nature for?
Money hungry, power hungry, self-serving bigotry?

To hell with that ignorance, based on that geometry
of shame.

I'm going back to nature.
I'm leaving this concrete,
pollutant,
money driven metropolis behind.

I'm going back to nature,
where this skin
doesn't mean anything.

*Inspired by Ras Kass *Nature of the Threat*

Dan Suelo

I want to be you Dan Suelo.
Living in your cave.
You have gone back to Nature.

Dan Suelo,
his skin tanned,
lives in a cave in Utah.
Survives on road kill
and wild onions.

Even though it be the same god
    Inspires you and creationism,
you have gone back to nature,
you have devolved,
your skin means nothing,
and it must be a lonely bliss.

Release

release my anger on the page
unlock my ethereal cage
open up the prison doors
head slams down upon the floor
drool of depression escapes my mouth
into the trash bag. Out of the house.

Idiot Wind

What lurks in the heat?
What whispers do you hear from the air?
When a fight lurks in the swelter,
the fevered air permeates brainwaves,
manifesting in violence of dog fight.
Blood of puncture wound.
Dripping and boiling on the cement porch.
Staining, leaving tangible remembrances.
The torrid summer air carries recklessness.
Currents pushing discontent,
a defiant front moving southbound.
What is it about air intangible,
air abstract?
With the heat or cold or dark or solitude.
Air deliverer of emotional oxygen
What whispers do you hear from the air?
When the wind tickles your ears
and you stare into the fog,
and you think you hear wishes,
for a different life, or new love, or money, or sanity.
For speaking into the air may seem safe
except, what whispers do others hear in the air
when the wind tickles their ears?

Sharing Air

Do you know why Jews have such big noses?
Because Air is free.
A joke I've heard times, too many.
But I am Jewish.
Not that you would know,
unless I told you so,
and those jokes are just a different way
for you to say, kike.

Yeah, my skin is light,
but that's no reason for you to be impolite
and start spouting that nasty racist shit like I'm going
to understand.

My man, are you serious?
You must be delirious if you can't see past this skin.
Don't get me started on this skin, again
and don't call me friend and pretend we're tight
because we're both white, we're both light skinned.

You think we share some ancient bloodline and
therefore we share the same mindset,
but I'm not cool with ignorance
and I don't want to walk down this road with you.
Because you probably have something to say about Jews,
probably some nasty words you'll use,

the purpose of which are to abuse
and further your ignorant views on the world.
What will it take for you to realize this melting pot is
actually a stew?

The air you breathe is the air I breathe.

But it's too late for reprieve.
Your time has past, you've left me no choice
but to call you out in literature.
But I'm not leaving my words dusty on a bookshelf
for you to never read.

I'm taking it right to you
to embarrass you in the streets.
So what did you have to say about Jews?

Go ahead, pull that trigger, say all the words that
make me want to puke.
Give me a reason to fight,
to internalize this blight,
to let this anger brew.
But have no doubt, what this is about.
I will find you.

Because I have no patience to share the air.
I have no patience to placate your glare,
but what drives me insane

is that I'm painfully aware
that you are absolutely,
right.
You're so right.
The air is free.
It's free.

And as long as it remains free,
I plan on breathing as much goddamned air as I
possibly can.
And if my nose grows
as a result
of all the free air I am breathing,
so be it.

And you can look at me and place me in some
stereotype you have constructed in your mind
and that's fine.

Because I will never impinge on your right to believe.
I will never infringe on your right to free speech
and even though we will always disagree
that is what makes this free air,
so worth breathing.

Master Plan

I prefer to believe in a master plan,
that somewhere, some mythological creature,
or energy,
or creator,
has a plan for me.

I like to believe that everything I have ever done has
served some greater purpose.

I like to believe that my life is special and somehow,
without my cog in the machine, the machine will fail,
sputter out in a cloud of heavy white smoke and die.

Free will means taking responsibility for your actions.
Choices I made were mine and mine alone.
There is no one and nothing to blame, and that just doesn't
work for me.

Maybe the Mormons have it right.
Put it to a vote,
but the way I see it,
if God tells you to do something,
you better fucking do it.

I want to be part of a master plan.

I want to be programmed.
Every choice I make, excusable and justified.

You can't choose fate, because fate chooses you.
Not by choice.
By chance.

Mainly I cannot believe
she would stay with me
by choice.

Dead End

Stay distracted America.
Laugh as we sit on our ever growing asses.
Empty heads,
vacant eyed zombies,
transfixed by the flashy glowing opiates that surround us.

Off our shores,
in not-so distant lands,
the earth splits apart
devastating Nations.
Text the world HELPING to 6969
and donate a dollar to the cause.

We can tell our friends,
Hey I did my part! I texted for the disaster!
You texted for the disaster?
No, but you could imagine if I did.

Stay distracted America.
Lest we forget there are still bloodied boots on the ground.
Lest we forget that children, women and men are victims
of war no matter the side.
But hey, we voted someone in who said they'd do
something about war.
We did our part.

We can tell our friends, hey I did my part!
I voted for rhetoric I agreed with!
You voted?
No, but you could imagine if I did.

Stay distracted America.
Talk and laugh in offices around the country.
Surrounded by strangers you see more than
your own family.
Producing nothing.
Near water coolers, in kitchens, in cubicles,
in suits with fancy ties and deadened eyes.
Talk about things that really matter.
Sports, celebrities, and the news.
You watch the news?
No, but you could
imagine if I did.
You could imagine.

Thirst

Your liquid passes my throat
coating my stomach
easing the pangs of apathy.
My soul emulsifies,
thickened by your thought,
your scent,
your concept.
Do songs contain truth?
Prove crooners wrong?
Tell me yes,
it doesn't matter what language.

Those damned butterflies in the pit of my stomach,
fluttering for tomorrow,
where she will exist,
as I exist,
co-existing on romantic plane.
Her image iconoclastically enshrined.
There are those god-damned butterflies again!
My mushroom of knowledge
somewhere in between
excited and frightened
wanes in the dark, cold, early morning,
underneath shining stars,
wishing it was storming.

I thirst for her energy,
to inspire me,
to drink her think.
I thirst for her sexuality,
my geometry of shame,
I thirst for her.
To drink her up,
baby, I drink you up.

Love Poem #69

My testicles are obstacles
we're numbers separated by infinitesimal decimals
I want you so bad I go to confessional
sit in the vestibule
and sputter obscenities

April Fool #3

Some of us grow too old, too quickly
Worn down by the world
Some of us lose our lust for life
With every drink
Every smoke

Escaping to worlds
Dimensions
Perceptions

Sitting in the midst of a thunderstorm
Light rain
Heavy wind
Lightning flashes

If I die for love,
Kill me.

Maria

At 2:30, in the darkness,
I yearn for her
sitting in my new pajamas and
pondering her essence.

She came strolling into my life smelling so good
and I thought
she's beyond me
and then we talked,
the click, connection,
stared deeply into her eyes,
attention paid.
Many have strolled in,
None have ever sung to me in Spanish.

April Fool #1

Drawn like on a canvas I am to you and
It's 4:00 and I am all out of cigarettes.
You're in Washington or Connecticut or New York.

There is a pounding on the surf.
The first splash angrily crashes.
Waves follow.
Angry little waves trying to suck you into the undertow.

Down you go into the confusion
It envelops you wholly.
Disbelief is your only child.
Sinking into hopelessness.
Your own arms driving you deeper into the void,
The sadness of the abyss seeps into your lungs.

Then somehow, you become aquatic,
You come up for just a little bit of air and
it's just enough to keep you from dying.

Ah,
Billy Joel,
we sing the same lovesick songs, my friend.
Allen, I am lost in the total Animal soup of time.
My dear April fool.

Not Zombie Love

Simply put;
I crave your naked flesh.
Not the way a zombie craves brains,
chasing you around with some vapid look in my eyes,
more like the way a dog craves his treat,
wide-eyed and drooling.

Time Study

I love her most in the morning,
shortly after waking,
while she is still sleeping,
and the early morn is hushed in silence.

Every day, I'm thankful yet another sun
                          has risen over our union,
that the birds keep singing our songs.

As the grass lays on its side and
            clear-skied moonlight
                washes

                      over

                            us,
I love her most.
        She doesn't even know I am awake,
                has no idea I'm watching her.

In these moments,
after coffee has been made,
after social media,
after the weather checked,
and the impending night draws closer,
which has me worried about
jobless,
moneyless,
homeless.

In these moments,
I am empowered
by her love,
by adoring her.

If that makes the afternoon sound terrible
by comparison:
Morning,
                like all other constructs of time,
is a state of mind
                      and often
        she sleeps past noon.

Olfactory Musings

You say I only write poems about you when you're mad.
This poem is to prove you absolutely and unequivocally wrong,
because sometimes i write poems when I'm mad.

It was a Wednesday.
nothing special about it.
No holiday to celebrate or event to commemorate,
just Wednesday.

I felt like I hadn't seen you in a month.
We had places to do
things to be
situations to be in.
For five to eight hours each night,
we slept next to each other,
our limbs entangled,
feeding off each other's heat.
but when the next days' sun would arise,
we would again be off our separate ways.

That is not a relationship, it is cohabitation,
and I did not sign up for cohabitation.
I would recall my college years and gasp
remembering the pathway of clothes

to get a glass of water from the kitchen
if there was a glass worthy of drinking,
all the swarthiness of a young bachelor
and that lifestyle more or less continued until you and I
became something else.

You give me a reason to be responsible
and to have pride in myself
And that's what I signed up for.
I want a reason to do the dishes or vacuum the floor,
because honestly, I still don't care what I think of me,
but I care what you think of me.
And we weren't around each other enough for me to be
thought of by you and it went like this for some time.

Wednesday, the Wednesday, the random nothing special
about it just the fourth day of the week
Wednesday
something happened.

The door opened,
and in you walked,
and I breathed you in,
and I got drunk.
I was drunk off your smell
and there was no scientific reason that something
my olfactory senses interpreted would cause such
physical elevation

and yet,
I would take a breath and inhale you, and it made
my brain float about inside my head
and even now I can still smell you
a part of me, entrenched in memory, never out of mind.

And this was sometime ago, and you and I are not
fighting
and you are not mad
but I am madly in love
and still drunk
and in my head, it's always Wednesday.

Color by Numbers

It's with you my life is blazing and amazing,
burning hot orange like a cigarette cherry
and when I stop to contemplate how we're raising kids,
I realize I have no fears,
this is how you make me feel.

How you make me feel can only be described in color,
fantastical and amazing,
because when I cause you stress
my sadness is azure like a lone ship on a desolate
seascape,

And when I am unsure and scared
I am maize dried corn, shrivelled and waiting to be
revealed by your hands

You send my mind constantly tripping over lush
hedge bushes
searching for that golden light at the end of the tunnel,
that beautiful, incandescent light of understanding,

And yes, I too get mad, and when my blood boils,
it boils magenta as bubbling blood in an apocalypse
brook
but never dark, never still,

because with you I have no fears,
this is how you make me feel.

And so, to you I offer the rainbow of my existence,
the full blown color of my soul,
Paint a picture, use a pointillism format,
millions of brightly colored dots combining into one
grand masterpiece.

My trust in you is beyond smokey charcoal grey,
it is earthen stone.
With you I have no fears, this is how you make me
feel.

What Have I Done?

What have I done
to make you act like this?
Alone and crying in the shower,
naked and full of despair.
Never in a million years would I have chosen this result.
I can't help but wonder,
to what fault
have I committed, instigated,
what behaviors have you placated?
I only know fear and sorrow and remorse,
and can only ponder the course
that this path of night cold and dark will bring.

April Fool #5

I.
To be on the receiving end of a kiss from the woman
you adore.
To be dizzied.
To hold her in my arms.
To cry happiness and regret.

April Fool, what's the point of being bitter?

To be melted.
To be reduced to thirteen years by the squeeze
of your palm.
To cherish.
To make love.
To love.

April Fool, how long is eternity?
Forever,
relative to now,
a concept of time,
which does not exist.

Eternity is,
before we met,
before we looked deep,

before we learned,
not to be afraid
Of you.
Of now.
Of forever.
Of me.

II.
Moments,
little moments in the grand scale of life.
A twisted bottle filled with sand
slowly counting out the last of our seconds.
The tick tick ticking of the clock.
The pit pit patter of the heart.
My almond beauty,
queen of our mystical universe,
take me in your arms and let me sleep,
pozhaluysta, my eyes grow tired of disbelief.

III.
We grow distant, you grow distant.
You are leaving soon.

April Fool #4

A chilly summer day
in the midst of midwestern heat
sheets of rain exploded on my windshield.

One way or another
someone in Kansas is sad,
and I'm terrified to know the truth.

One way or another,
one way or another,
I hope for one way, not another,
one way or another.

April Fool #6

Is tonight the night I will finally see you, my dearest?
Long it has been since my eyes cast a frivolous glance
in your direction.
What if there are tears?
What if you smile and I melt?
What if I freak out?
What if I feel nothing at all?
Is tonight the night I will finally feel you, my dearest?
Long it has been since my arms wrapped a chivalrous squeeze upon your body.
I wonder if my love will come freely?
I have been jumbled,
out of proportion,
unfocused,
waiting for your imminent return,
into my immediate vicinity,
into my reality
and yet sometimes, it's like, who?
Consequence of passing time, I suppose.
No, tonight is the night
I will go to the fridge and
substitute kool-aide for love.
Tomorrow at three a.m.
for no apparent reason,
my heart may call out to her.
I will ball up on my bed,
under my covers,
with the fan blowing in my face,
and I will hope to dream.

Deadbeat

It's weird having a father
who lives less than fifteen minutes from you
and doesn't have the time or inclination
to send you the very best, or make an effort,
if you want the entire truth of it.

I called him today at 3:22 p.m.
and he wasn't home.
So I left a message,
and he won't return my call.

I'm not stupid.
He'll blow it off.

It's a shame, because if he doesn't call back
    today,
he may never know,
he has a grandson.

A Poem for My Mother

I wasn't raised in the ghetto
I was raised in the suburbs.

We weren't rich but had food in the cupboards.
My school was mostly white weren't a lot of colors,
and some say there were kids who had butlers.

I didn't have to fight in order to survive,
but I did have to write to try and get by.
I had a lot of anger brewing deep inside,
I took out on the curbside.

Firecracked my GI Joes
at three bills a pop I did not know
the value of a dollar at thirteen years old,
blew up half my toys just to watch them go.
Sold the other half a nickel a piece.
My mom was so mad she couldn't believe.

How the hell could I be so irresponsible?
My independence she'd have to pull.

But that would have been too hard,
because she was working 3 jobs,
while I smoked weed through glass
and blew off my class.

All the learning gone in a haze of smoke.
Like so many others, viewed school as one big joke.
Barely scraped by, barely graduated.
Got a girl pregnant before I skated
off to college where no one could find me,
more of the same, spending mama's money.
Chased girls, bought weed, coke and LSD.

So there I was at eighteen doing drugs,
Hung out with people pretended I'm a thug,
acted like a badass pretended I was tough,
made up shit so my life would sound rough.

Oh yeah let me tell ya must have been hard,
I mean for god sakes I had to buy my own car.
Never mind she paid my insurance,
and whenever I need a lift she was there for assurance.
What's the pay back for all her kindness?
So many years full of dumb blindness.

Unable to see this is how you live.
Always putting off her own dreams to better off her kids.

A few years later when I was on my own,
I called up my mom on the telephone.
Once again, I ask to borrow money.
She didn't even think before she gave it to me.

Money comes easy,
support does not.
She gave freely.
One day I hope to be
half the woman she is to me.

Because that's the type of woman that she is,
never put herself in front of her kids.
For the longest time I never appreciated
all the sacrifices she must have made.

It's been over ten years since I was 18
now I got kids who are looking up to me
most of my mistakes I tried to eradicate
and for some of them I hope I'm not too late
I got a son who is just getting to know me
and a baby mamma who owns about half of me
but in the end it's only money
and the lesson was well taught it's kinda funny

because I finally put my kids in front of myself
put those selfish ways up on the shelf.

I had a chance to live my dream
I just didn't know what the dream was,
and now that I'm submersed
I realize how much my family is worth
The lessons mama taught are still with me
and for that I'm grateful eternally.

Deadbeat #2

He doesn't love me.
He doesn't respect me.
He spends all day wishing I am not who I am.
He expresses only shame and negativity around me.
His memories are only sad and sick.
He wishes I wasn't blood.
He wishes I wasn't his blood.
He wishes I wasn't his father.

King idiot they call me.
King of the assholes.
King of the deadbeat dads.
Even though I pay.
Even though I fight.
Even though I love.
Deadbeat because I am not there.
Haven't been there.

He doesn't trust me.

Who could blame him?
I wasn't there when he was little.
I wasn't there when he instinctively would have trusted.
I wasn't there.

Our Story

The best decision
I ever made,
at the time,
created pain

and separation

and stress
and sadness.

The best decision
I ever made,
at the time,
created hardship
and harsh words
and hassles.

The best decision
I ever made,
eventually led,
to glee
and growth
and gratitude.

He was 10,
I sued for the right to be more than
biology,
to be Dad,
to be there.

15 years later
the best decision
I ever made
is still
the best decision
I
ever
made.

Jas Abramowitz is a writer, actor, and performance poet. He is originally from Kansas City, MO and spent seven years in Chicago, IL before moving to Jacksonville, Florida in 2015. His poetry performance credits include four years as part of OPUS, a memorized poetry performance group in Kansas City, and is a 3 time winner of Chicago's Green Mill Poetry Slam.

This project was made possible, in part, by generous support from the Osage Arts Community.

Osage Arts Community provides temporary time, space and support for the creation of new artistic works in a retreat format, serving creative people of all kinds — visual artists, composers, poets, fiction and nonfiction writers. Located on a 152-acre farm in an isolated rural mountainside setting in Central Missouri and bordered by ¾ of a mile of the Gasconade River, OAC provides residencies to those working alone, as well as welcoming collaborative teams, offering living space and workspace in a country environment to emerging and mid-career artists. For more information, visit us at www.osageac.org